— *a Gift* —

for: _____

from: _____

date: _____

THE PRICE OF

Freedom

BY MICHAEL W. SMITH

WITH WENDY LEE NENTWIG

J COUNTRYMAN

Nashville, Tennessee
www.jcountryman.com

Unless otherwise indicated, all Scripture quotations in this book are from the New King James Version of the Bible (NKJV) ®, copyright © 1979, 1980, 1982, Thomas Nelson, Inc., Publishers.

The New American Standard Bible (NASB) © 1960, 1962, 1963, 1971, 1972, 1973, 1975, and 1977 by the Lockman Foundation, and are used by permission.

The New International Version of the Bible (NIV) © 1984 by the International Bible Society. Used by permission of Zondervan Bible Publishers.

J. Countryman® is a trademark of Thomas Nelson, Inc.

Design: Anderson Thomas Design, Inc.

Project Editor: Kathy Baker

Photography: © PhotoDisc, © Comstock, © EyeWire, © Digital Stock Professional, © Anderson Thomas Design, Inc. Special thanks to Larry Hicklen.

ISBN 0-8499-5609-9

Printed and bound in the United States of America

www.thomasnelson.com

Contents

We have a place, all of us, in a long story . . . the story of a slave-holding society that became a servant of freedom. . . . It is the American story; a story of flawed and fallible people, united across the generations by grand and enduring ideals.

President George W. Bush in his inaugural address, January 20, 2001

INTRODUCTION

THE ATTACKS ON SEPTEMBER 11, 2001, SHOOK THE UNITED STATES OF AMERICA to its core, but the fear and anger those events fueled soon gave way to a new surge of patriotism. We came to value freedom more when were reminded that others want to destroy it. From under the rubble we unearthed a new love for our country. Flags flew. Anthems rang. People reached out to neighbors and strangers alike. And we realized that we are willing to pay almost any price—with our time, our money, and even our lives—to protect our country and preserve our freedom.

This is a terrible, wonderful time in history. Every generation faces challenges to freedom and now it is our turn. But along with the responsibility, there is also much to celebrate. This book takes an inspirational look at the honor of being an American—especially a Christian American—and the price paid by the brave men and women who left us this legacy of freedom.

Freedom's History

Yesterday, the greatest question was decided which ever was debated in America; and a greater perhaps never was, nor will be, decided among men. A resolution was passed without one dissenting colony, that those United Colonies are, and of right ought to be, free and independent States.

John Adams in a letter to his wife, July 3, 1776

The area where I make my home with my family is filled with reminders of freedom.

Civil War markers dot the landscape here in Franklin, Tennessee, and century-old stray bullets have been discovered right in my front yard.

The bloody Battle of Franklin is not just a memory. Books continue to bring the story to life, and local groups stage re-enactments so we won't forget what has gone before. Then there are the cemeteries—constant reminders of the price of freedom.

We studied these events in history class, but to walk daily on the ground where it took place makes it real in a way a musty textbook never can. That's probably why, as I sat down to my piano to compose music for an instrumental release, the theme of "freedom" emerged.

The song "Freedom" was inspired directly by living

> "…As I sat down to my piano to compose music for an instrumental release, the theme of 'freedom' emerged."

amid such history. You can't help but wonder what it was really like during that time period. Of course, the fighting was intense and there were massive casualties, but as the music came to life, I imagined a more hopeful scene: A young man walking home at the end of the war. He was one of the lucky ones whose life had been spared. He had fought for freedom and now he was returning to his family. He had survived the war, but war takes its toll on the survivors, too. He had paid a bitter price for our freedom.

— M.W.G.

*O*UR RELIANCE IS IN THE LOVE OF LIBERTY
WHICH GOD HAS PLANTED IN OUR BOSOMS. OUR DEFENSE IS
IN THE PRESERVATION OF THE SPIRIT WHICH PRIZED LIBERTY AS THE
HERITAGE OF ALL MEN, IN ALL LANDS, EVERYWHERE. DESTROY
THIS SPIRIT AND YOU HAVE PLANTED THE SEEDS OF DESPOTISM AROUND YOUR
OWN DOORS. FAMILIARIZE YOURSELF WITH THE CHAINS OF BONDAGE, AND
YOU ARE PREPARING YOUR OWN LIMBS TO WEAR THEM.

Abraham Lincoln in a speech given in Edwardsville, Illinois, 1858

*F*OUR SCORE AND SEVEN YEARS AGO
OUR FATHERS BROUGHT FORTH ON THIS CONTINENT A NEW NATION,
CONCEIVED IN LIBERTY, AND DEDICATED TO THE PROPOSITION THAT
ALL MEN ARE CREATED EQUAL."

President Abraham Lincoln, "The Gettysburg Address," November 19, 1863

14

I SHALL NEVER SURRENDER NOR RETREAT. THEN, I CALL ON YOU IN THE NAME OF LIBERTY, OF PATRIOTISM, AND OF EVERYTHING DEAR TO THE AMERICAN CHARACTER, TO COME TO OUR AID WITH ALL DISPATCH. THE ENEMY IS RECEIVING REINFORCEMENTS DAILY AND WILL NO DOUBT INCREASE TO THREE OR FOUR THOUSAND IN FOUR OR FIVE DAYS. IF THIS CALL IS NEGLECTED, I AM DETERMINED TO SUSTAIN MYSELF AS LONG AS POSSIBLE AND DIE LIKE A SOLDIER WHO NEVER FORGETS WHAT IS DUE TO HIS OWN HONOR AND THAT OF HIS COUNTRY.

William Barrett Travis, Lieutenant Colonel at the Alamo,
written to "the people of Texas and all Americans in the world," February 24, 1836

Faith & Freedom

It was for freedom that Christ set us free.

Galatians 5:1 (NAS)

I can't think of freedom without remembering the sacrifice Jesus made on my behalf.

Personal freedom, political freedom—they pale in comparison to freedom in Christ. I could be imprisoned in chains, but still I'm a free man because of my faith. That's true freedom. No battle can change it, no government can revoke it. I've been set free.

— M.W.S.

*I*N NO OTHER WAY CAN THIS REPUBLIC BECOME A WORLD POWER IN THE NOBLEST SENSE OF THE WORD THAN BY PUTTING INTO HER LIFE AND THE LIVES OF HER CITIZENS THE SPIRIT AND PRINCIPLES OF THE GREAT FOUNDER OF CHRISTIANITY.

David J. Brewer, Associate Justice of the U. S. Supreme Court, 1889-1910

I AM SURE THERE NEVER WAS A PEOPLE WHO HAD MORE REASON TO ACKNOWLEDGE A DIVINE INTERPOSITION IN THEIR AFFAIRS THAN THOSE OF THE UNITED STATES.

George Washington to John Armstrong, March 11, 1792

*I*T CANNOT BE EMPHASIZED TOO STRONGLY OR TOO OFTEN THAT THIS GREAT NATION WAS FOUNDED, NOT BY RELIGIONISTS, BUT BY CHRISTIANS; NOT ON RELIGIONS, BUT ON THE GOSPEL OF JESUS CHRIST. FOR THIS VERY REASON PEOPLES OF OTHER FAITHS HAVE BEEN AFFORDED ASYLUM, PROSPERITY, AND FREEDOM OF WORSHIP HERE.

Patrick Henry

*O*F ALL THE DISPOSITIONS AND HABITS WHICH LEAD TO POLITICAL PROSPERITY, RELIGION AND MORALITY ARE INDISPENSABLE SUPPORTS. IT IS IMPOSSIBLE TO RIGHTLY GOVERN THE WORLD WITHOUT GOD AND THE BIBLE.

George Washington

*W*E HAVE NO GOVERNMENT ARMED WITH POWER CAPABLE OF CONTENDING WITH HUMAN PASSIONS UNBRIDLED BY MORALITY AND RELIGION. AVARICE, AMBITION, REVENGE, OR GALLANTRY WOULD BREAK THE STRONGEST CORDS OF OUR CONSTITUTION AS A WHALE GOES THROUGH A NET. OUR CONSTITUTION WAS MADE ONLY FOR A MORAL AND RELIGIOUS PEOPLE. IT IS WHOLLY INADEQUATE TO THE GOVERNMENT OF ANY OTHER.

John Adams

It's extremely important that our president be a spiritual leader.

In the difficult, uncertain time after the terrorist attacks on America, people looked to our president for direction, and what they saw was a godly man, a man with tremendous faith. George W. Bush provided amazing leadership for our country in his first year in the White House. His references to God and to faith and his quoting of Scripture still resound with power. People have been talking more about God, and prayer has suddenly become politically correct. The spiritual climate has shifted and I can't help but think our president's example has had something to do with that.

— M.W.G.

Freedom's Responsibility

America is a nation full of good fortune, with so much to be grateful for, but we are not spared from suffering. In every generation the world has produced enemies of human freedom. They have attacked us because we are freedom's home and defender, and the commitment of our fathers is now the calling of our time.

President George W. Bush in his National Day of Prayer & Remembrance address given at the National Cathedral in Washington, D.C., Sept. 14, 2001

*F*OR EVERYONE TO WHOM MUCH IS GIVEN,
FROM HIM MUCH WILL BE REQUIRED;
AND TO WHOM MUCH HAS BEEN COMMITTED,
OF HIM THEY WILL ASK THE MORE.

Luke 12:48

*A*CT AS A FREE MAN, AND DO NOT USE YOUR FREEDOM
AS A COVERING FOR EVIL, BUT USE IT AS BONDSLAVES OF GOD.

1 Peter 2:16 (NAS)

*P*ROVIDENCE HAS SHOWERED ON THIS FAVORED LAND BLESSINGS
WITHOUT NUMBER, AND HAS CHOSEN YOU AS THE GUARDIANS OF FREEDOM, TO
PRESERVE IT FOR THE BENEFIT OF THE HUMAN RACE. MAY HE WHO HOLDS IN
HIS HANDS THE DESTINIES OF NATIONS MAKE YOU WORTHY OF THE FAVORS
HE HAS BESTOWED AND ENABLE YOU, WITH PURE HEARTS AND PURE
HANDS AND SLEEPLESS VIGILANCE, TO GUARD AND DEFEND TO THE END OF
TIME THE GREAT CHARGE HE HAS COMMITTED TO YOUR KEEPING.

President Andrew Jackson in his farewell address on March 4, 1837

Here in America it's so easy to take our freedom for granted.

We see it as our birthright, as our entitlement. And yet when I look at what happens in other countries, it hits home: We're the freest nation in the world. And while it's difficult to constantly be aware of all that we have, seeing the lack of freedom that others experience makes me determined to be more thankful for the gift that is living in America.

— M.W.G.

DUTY. HONOR. COUNTRY.

DUTY. HONOR. COUNTRY. THOSE THREE HALLOWED WORDS REVERENTLY DICTATE WHAT YOU WANT TO BE, WHAT YOU CAN BE, WHAT YOU WILL BE. THEY ARE YOUR RALLYING POINT, TO BUILD COURAGE WHEN COURAGE SEEMS TO FAIL, TO REGAIN FAITH WHEN THERE SEEMS TO be little cause for faith, to create hope when hope becomes forlorn. . . .

The unbelievers will say they are but words, but a slogan, but a flamboyant phrase. Every pedant, every demagogue, every cynic, every hypocrite, every troublemaker, and—I am sorry to say—some others of an entirely different character, will try to downgrade them even to the extent of mockery and ridicule. But these are some of the things they do: They build your basic character. They mold you for your future roles as the custodians of the nation's defense. They make you strong enough to know when you are weak and brave enough to face yourself when you are afraid.

They teach you to be proud and unbending in honest failure, but humble and gentle in success; not to substitute words for actions, not to seek the path of comfort, but to face the stress and spur of difficulty and challenge; to learn to stand up in the storm, but to have compassion on those who fail; to master yourself before you seek to master others; to have a heart that is clean, a goal that is high; to learn to laugh yet never forget how to weep; to reach into the future, yet never neglect the past; to be serious, yet never to take yourself too seriously; to be modest so that you will remember the simplicity of true greatness, the open mind of true wisdom, the meekness of true strength.

They give you a temperate will, a quality of imagination, a vigor of the emotions, a freshness of the deep springs of life, a temperamental predominance of courage over timidity, an appetite for adventure over love of ease.

They create in your heart the sense of wonder, the unfailing hope of what next, and the joy and inspiration of life. They teach you in this way to be an officer and a gentleman.

General Douglas MacArthur in a speech delivered at West Point, May 12, 1962. To this day, each new cadet receives a copy of this address.

*O*NLY A **VIRTUOUS PEOPLE** ARE
CAPABLE OF FREEDOM. AS NATIONS BECOME CORRUPT AND VICIOUS,
THEY HAVE MORE NEED OF MASTERS.

Benjamin Franklin

A **BIBLE** AND A NEWSPAPER IN EVERY HOUSE,
A GOOD SCHOOL IN EVERY DISTRICT——ALL STUDIED AND APPRECIATED
AS THEY MERIT——ARE THE PRINCIPLE SUPPORT OF VIRTUE, MORALITY,
AND **CIVIL LIBERTY.**

Benjamin Franklin, March 1778

*N*o people ought to feel greater obligations to CELEBRATE THE GOODNESS of the Great Disposer of events and the Destiny of Nations than the people of the United States . . . And to the same DIVINE AUTHOR of every good and perfect gift we are indebted for all those privileges and advantages, religious as well as civil, which are so richly enjoyed in THIS FAVORED LAND.

James Madison, signer of the Federal Constitution and 4th President of the United States

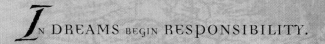

*I*n DREAMS begin RESPONSIBILITY.

William Butler Yeats

The torch has been passed to a new generation..

The world is very different now. For man holds in his mortal hands the power to abolish all forms of human poverty and all forms of human life. And yet the same revolutionary beliefs for which our forebears fought are still at issue around the globe—the belief that the rights of man come not from the generosity of the state but from the hand of God.

We dare not forget today that we are the heirs of that first revolution. Let the word go forth from this time and place, to friend and foe alike, that the torch has been passed to a new generation of Americans—born in this century, tempered by war, disciplined by a hard and bitter peace, proud of our ancient heritage—and unwilling to witness or permit the slow undoing of

30

those human rights to which this nation has always been committed, and to which we are committed today at home and around the world.

Let every nation know, whether it wishes us well or ill, that we shall pay any price, bear any burden, meet any hardship, support any friend, oppose any foe to assure the survival and the success of liberty. This much we pledge—and more.

John F. Kennedy, in his inaugural address, January 20, 1961

Let every nation know, whether it wishes us well or ill, that we shall pay any price, bear any burdern, meet any hardship, support any friend, oppose any foe to assure the survival and the success of liberty.

A person gets from a symbol the meaning he puts into it.

United States Supreme Court, June 14, 1943

PLEDGE OF ALLEGIANCE

I pledge allegiance to the flag of the United States of America and to the Republic for which it stands, one nation, under God, indivisible, with liberty and justice for all.

THE AMERICAN'S CREED

I BELIEVE IN THE UNITED STATES OF AMERICA
AS A GOVERNMENT OF THE PEOPLE, BY THE PEOPLE, FOR THE PEOPLE;
WHOSE JUST POWERS ARE DERIVED FROM THE CONSENT OF THE GOVERNED;
A DEMOCRACY IN A REPUBLIC, A SOVEREIGN NATION OF MANY SOVEREIGN STATES;
A PERFECT UNION, ONE AND INSEPARABLE, ESTABLISHED UPON THOSE
PRINCIPLES OF FREEDOM, EQUALITY, JUSTICE, AND HUMANITY FOR WHICH
AMERICAN PATRIOTS SACRIFICED THEIR LIVES AND FORTUNES.
I THEREFORE BELIEVE IT IS MY DUTY TO MY COUNTRY TO
LOVE IT; TO SUPPORT ITS CONSTITUTION; TO OBEY ITS LAWS;
TO RESPECT ITS FLAG; AND TO DEFEND IT AGAINST ALL ENEMIES.

*Written by William Tyler Page in 1918 as the winning entry in an essay contest
to develop an American Creed*

The Fourth of July.

For most Americans that day means fireworks and cookouts, and my family is
no exception. Almost every year we celebrate our country's freedom in
Beaver Creek, Colorado, where we watch an incredible fireworks display. But
in the midst of all the celebrating, we always take time to talk about the
price that's been paid for freedom. As a family, we talk of the people who went
before us and the sacrifices they made. That provides some important perspective
that would otherwise be lost in the frenzy to get to the fireworks, and
it keeps us from losing sight of what
we're really celebrating.

— M.W.G.

the Story of Betsy Ross

ELIZABETH GRISCOM (CALLED BETSY) WAS BORN IN PENNSYLVANIA ON NEW YEAR'S DAY, 1752, INTO A PROMINENT QUAKER FAMILY. UPON FINISHING SCHOOL, SHE APPRENTICED AS AN UPHOLSTERER, BUT HER QUIET LIFE WAS TURNED UPSIDE DOWN WHEN, AT AGE 21, SHE ELOPED with fellow apprentice, John Ross, an Episcopalian. No longer welcome at the Quaker meeting house, Betsy attended Christ Church with her husband, sitting in a pew across the aisle from George Washington.

As the American Revolution began, John joined the war effort and soon made Betsy a widow. It was only a few months later that Betsy attended the meeting that would secure her place in history. George Washington, Robert Morris, and George Ross, the uncle of her late husband, came to Betsy's home in May 1776 and asked her to create a flag. It wasn't the first time Washington had come to Betsy in need of a tailor; she had embroidered the ruffles and cuffs of several of his garments. As the meeting got under way, the men shared with Betsy the design they had in mind, and she added her own touches, changing their six-point stars to the five-point variety we still see today.

The flag was finished barely a month before the Declaration of Independence was read aloud for the first time at Philadelphia's Independence Hall, where the Liberty Bell's ringing signaled the birth of a new, free nation.

The battle was far from over, however. Betsy would lose another husband to the Revolution and be forced to house British soldiers in her home during the war. She also put her sewing skills to use creating more practical items, like the cloth pouches that the Continental soldiers used to carry their gunpowder.

At the end of the war, Betsy's work and sacrifice weren't forgotten. On June 14, 1777, Betsy's handiwork was adopted as the national flag by the Continental Congress and has flown proudly ever since.

THE NEW COLOSSUS

Not like the brazen giant of Greek fame,
With conquering limbs astride from land to land;
Here at our sea-washed, sunset gates shall stand
A mighty woman with a torch,
Whose flame is the imprisoned lightning
And her name Mother of Exiles.
From her beacon hand glows world-wide welcome;
Her mild eyes command the air-bridged harbor that twin cities frame.
'Keep, ancient lands, your storied pomp!' cries she with silent lips.
Give me your tired, your poor,
Your huddled masses yearning to breathe free,
The wretched refuse of your teeming shore,
Send these, the homeless, tempest-tost to me,
I lift my lamp beside the golden door.

Emma Lazarus, written to help raise funds for construction of the Statue of Liberty's pedestal in 1903.
The statue itself was designated a National Monument on October 15, 1924.

*T*HE FLAG . . . IS A VISIBLE SYMBOL OF THE IDEAL ASPIRATIONS OF THE AMERICAN PEOPLE. IT IS THE ONE FOCUS IN WHICH ALL UNITE IN REVERENTIAL DEVOTION. WE DIFFER IN RELIGION; WE DIFFER IN POLITICS; WE ENGAGE IN DISPUTES AS TO THE TRUE MEANING OF THE CONSTITUTION, AND EVEN CHALLENGE THE WISDOM OF SOME OF ITS PROVISIONS; WE INJECT SELF-INTEREST AND CUPIDITY INTO MOST OF THE ORDINARY TRANSACTIONS OF DAILY LIFE, BUT THROUGH THE SANCTIFYING FOLDS OF THE FLAG, THE COLLECTIVE INTELLIGENCE OF THE NATION RISES SUPERIOR TO THE WISDOM OF ITS PARTS, AND THUS ENSURES THE PERPETUITY OF THE REPUBLIC.

Major General Arthur MacArthur

*O*UR FLAG IS A NATIONAL ENSIGN, PURE AND SIMPLE, BEHOLD IT! LISTEN TO IT! EVERY STAR HAS A TONGUE, EVERY STRIPE IS ARTICULATE.

Massachusetts Senator Robert C. Winthrop (1809-1894)

the Star-Spangled Banner

(verses 1 & 4)

Oh, SAY CAN YOU SEE BY THE DAWN'S EARLY LIGHT

What SO PROUDLY WE HAILED AT THE TWILIGHT'S LAST GLEAMING?

Whose BROAD STRIPES AND BRIGHT STARS THROUGH THE PERILOUS FIGHT,

O'ER THE RAMPARTS WE WATCHED WERE SO GALLANTLY STREAMING?

And THE ROCKETS' RED GLARE, THE BOMBS BURSTING IN AIR

Gave PROOF THROUGH THE NIGHT THAT OUR FLAG WAS STILL THERE

Oh, SAY DOES THAT STAR-SPANGLED BANNER YET WAVE

O'ER THE LAND OF THE FREE AND THE HOME OF THE BRAVE?

OH! THUS BE IT EVER, WHEN FREEMEN SHALL STAND

    BETWEEN THEIR LOVED HOMES AND THE WAR'S DESOLATION!

BLEST WITH VICTORY AND PEACE, MAY THE HEAVEN-RESCUED LAND

    PRAISE THE POWER THAT HATH MADE AND PRESERVED US A NATION.

THEN CONQUER WE MUST, FOR OUR CAUSE IT IS JUST,

    AND THIS BE OUR MOTTO: "IN GOD IS OUR TRUST."

AND THE STAR-SPANGLED BANNER FOREVER SHALL WAVE

    O'ER THE LAND OF THE FREE AND THE HOME OF THE BRAVE!

penned by Francis Scott Key, during the defense of Baltimore's Fort McHenry, September 20, 1814

Originally written as a poem, "The Star-Spangled Banner" was later set to music with Congress finally naming it the national anthem in 1931, securing forever the status of the flag it celebrated as a beloved symbol of freedom. The actual flag that inspired the national anthem passed through the hands of many members of a prominent Baltimore family before being donated to the Smithsonian Institution, where it is being preserved.

Freedom's Price

Since this country was founded, each generation of Americans has been summoned to give testimony to its national loyalty. The graves of young Americans who answered the call to service surround the globe.

President John F. Kennedy, inaugural address, January 20, 1961

I remember when President Kennedy was shot.

I was six and even my child-mind grasped the enormity of it: Our president's been assassinated! Five years later, when Robert Kennedy was also gunned down, I was old enough to understand, but still young enough that I cried myself to sleep. Here was a young, charismatic man who I knew could have been our next president, and then he was just gone. I remember having so many questions.

My mom came up to check on me that night, but I couldn't speak. What words could I possibly find to encompass all that we were feeling? The price some pay for freedom is beyond comprehension. It was certainly beyond the articulation of a young boy.

— M.W.G.

THESE ARE THE TIMES THAT TRY MEN'S SOULS. THE SUMMER SOLDIER AND THE SUNSHINE PATRIOT WILL, IN THIS CRISIS, SHRINK FROM THE SERVICE OF THEIR COUNTRY; BUT HE THAT STANDS IT NOW, DESERVES THE LOVE AND THANKS OF MAN AND WOMAN. TYRANNY, LIKE HELL, IS NOT EASILY CONQUERED; YET WE HAVE THIS CONSOLATION WITH US, THAT THE HARDER THE CONFLICT, THE MORE GLORIOUS THE TRIUMPH. WHAT WE OBTAIN TOO CHEAP, WE ESTEEM TOO LIGHTLY: IT IS DEARNESS ONLY THAT GIVES EVERY THING ITS VALUE. HEAVEN KNOWS HOW TO PUT A PROPER PRICE UPON ITS GOODS; AND IT WOULD BE STRANGE INDEED IF SO CELESTIAL AN ARTICLE AS FREEDOM SHOULD NOT BE HIGHLY RATED. . . .

Thomas Paine, written during one of the American Revolution's gloomiest hours

*I*T IS A FEARFUL THING TO LEAD THIS GREAT PEACEFUL PEOPLE INTO WAR . . . BUT THE RIGHT IS MORE PRECIOUS THAN PEACE, AND WE SHALL FIGHT FOR THE THINGS WHICH WE HAVE ALWAYS CARRIED NEAREST OUR HEARTS—FOR DEMOCRACY, FOR THE RIGHT OF THOSE WHO SUBMIT TO AUTHORITY TO HAVE A VOICE IN THEIR OWN GOVERNMENTS, FOR THE RIGHTS AND LIBERTIES OF SMALL NATIONS, FOR A UNIVERSAL DOMINION OF RIGHT BY SUCH A CONCERT OF FREE PEOPLES AS SHALL BRING PEACE AND SAFETY TO ALL NATIONS AND MAKE THE WORLD ITSELF AT LAST FREE.

President Woodrow Wilson in a speech before Congress as he requested a declaration of war in 1917, leading the United States of America into World War I

*T*HOSE WHO EXPECT TO REAP THE BLESSINGS OF FREEDOM
MUST, LIKE MEN, UNDERGO THE FATIGUE OF SUPPORTING IT.

Thomas Paine

*T*HEY THAT CAN GIVE UP ESSENTIAL LIBERTY TO OBTAIN A LITTLE
TEMPORARY SAFETY DESERVE NEITHER LIBERTY NOR SAFETY.

Benjamin Franklin

Freedom's
Heroes

Is life so dear, or peace so sweet as to be purchased at the price of chains and slavery? Forbid it, Almighty God! I know not what course others may take; but as for me, give me liberty or give me death!

Patrick Henry, in a speech before the Virginia Assembly, March 23, 1775

Most people are fortunate if they meet one hero in their lifetime, but I've been blessed to spend time with several.

I'm inspired every time I'm a guest of Billy Graham at one of his crusades; he continues to push on tirelessly for the faith even after all these years. I've been fortunate to know former presidents Carter, Ford, Reagan, and Bush; my respect for these men is tremendous. And then there's Captain Scott O'Grady, who survived nearly six days after being shot down over Bosnia. I've come to call him a friend. During a huge Fourth of July event in Dallas with more than 100,000 people in attendance I got to introduce Scott. When he finally came out, the place just went crazy in a way that was different from the reception given to a recording artist or a celebrity. They knew they were seeing a modern-day hero.

Still, not all heroes are well-known. Most are of the small-town variety—those who are in the trenches every day trying to rescue others, people who have had a great impact on their communities. I think of people like my dear friend Joe White, who runs the Kanakuk Kamps and is a hero to thousands of kids. I think of friends like Lucy Freed, who stood in the gap for hundreds and hundreds of unborn children here in Nashville. And then there's my dad. He's definitely my hero for the way he's raised us and loved us, and for the way he still loves my mom more than the whole world. He's been a great example and isn't that, more than anything, what a hero is?

— *M.W.S.*

*N*EVER IN THE FIELD OF HUMAN CONFLICT WAS
SO MUCH OWED BY SO MANY TO SO FEW.

*Winston Churchill, August 20, 1940, referring to the airmen
whose brave flying turned the tide of World War II*

*C*OURAGE IS RIGHTLY ESTEEMED THE FIRST OF HUMAN QUALITIES
BECAUSE IT IS THE QUALITY WHICH GUARANTEES ALL OTHERS.

Winston Churchill

A NATION, AS A SOCIETY, FORMS A MORAL PERSON,
AND EVERY MEMBER OF IT IS PERSONALLY RESPONSIBLE
FOR HIS SOCIETY.

Thomas Jefferson, written to George Hammond, 1792

*G*OOD GOVERNMENT GENERALLY BEGINS IN THE FAMILY, AND IF
THE MORAL CHARACTER OF A PEOPLE ONCE DEGENERATE, THEIR POLITICAL
CHARACTER MUST SOON FOLLOW.

*Elias Boudinot, president of the Continental Congress, later a congressman from New Jersey,
also president of the American Bible Society*

There is a current in history and it runs toward freedom.

President George W. Bush in his address to the United Nations, Nov. 10, 2001

I do not shrink from this responsibility—I welcome it.

IN THE LONG HISTORY OF THE WORLD, ONLY A FEW GENERATIONS HAVE BEEN GRANTED THE ROLE OF DEFENDING FREEDOM IN ITS HOUR OF MAXIMUM DANGER. I DO NOT SHRINK FROM THIS RESPONSIBILITY—I WELCOME IT. I DO NOT BELIEVE THAT ANY OF US WOULD EXCHANGE PLACES with any other people or any other generation. The energy, the faith, the devotion which we bring to this endeavor will light our country and all who serve it—and the glow from that fire can truly light the world.

And so, my fellow Americans: Ask not what your country can do for you, ask what you can do for your country. My fellow citizens of the world: Ask not what America will do for you, but what together we can do for the freedom of man. . . . With a good conscience our only sure reward, with history the final judge of our deeds, let us go forth to lead the land we love, asking His blessing and His help, but knowing that here on earth God's work must truly be our own.

President John F. Kennedy in his inaugural address, January 20, 1961

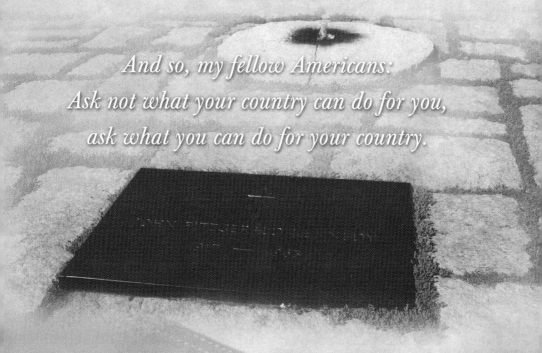

And so, my fellow Americans:
Ask not what your country can do for you,
ask what you can do for your country.

*W*E DID NOT ASK FOR **THIS MISSION**, YET THERE IS HONOR
IN HISTORY'S CALL. WE HAVE A CHANCE TO WRITE THE STORY OF OUR TIMES,
A STORY OF COURAGE DEFEATING CRUELTY AND LIGHT OVERCOMING
DARKNESS. THIS CALLING IS WORTHY OF ANY LIFE AND WORTHY OF EVERY NATION.

President George W. Bush in his speech to the United Nations, November 10, 2001

*T*HE ONLY THING NECESSARY FOR THE TRIUMPH OF EVIL
IS FOR GOOD MEN TO DO NOTHING.

Edmund Burke

We HOLD THESE TRUTHS TO BE SELF-EVIDENT, THAT ALL MEN ARE CREATED EQUAL, THAT THEY ARE ENDOWED BY THEIR CREATOR WITH CERTAIN UNALIENABLE RIGHTS, THAT AMONG THESE ARE LIFE, LIBERTY AND THE PURSUIT OF HAPPINESS.

The Unanimous Declaration of the Thirteen United States of America, July 4, 1776

Hold ON, MY FRIENDS, TO THE CONSTITUTION AND TO THE REPUBLIC FOR WHICH IT STANDS. MIRACLES DO NOT CLUSTER AND WHAT HAS HAPPENED ONCE IN 6,000 YEARS MAY NOT HAPPEN AGAIN. HOLD ON TO THE CONSTITUTION, FOR IF THE AMERICAN CONSTITUTION SHOULD FAIL, THERE WILL BE ANARCHY THROUGHOUT THE WORLD.

Daniel Webster, 1851

CONCLUSION

FREEDOM IS NOT JUST OUR HERITAGE; IT'S OUR BIRTHRIGHT. BUT FREEDOM HAS A PRICE. Every generation of Americans has fought its own battles to secure or preserve the freedoms we enjoy. And we will continue to defend the precious gift our forefathers gave us so that we, too, can leave a legacy of freedom to our children. There will be struggles and setbacks, our own price to pay, but we will prevail. Future generations will remain free to pursue their dreams and live out their destinies in the world and in Christ until His return. And as we seek Him, may God truly bless America.

MICHAEL W. SMITH'S FREEDOM, THE HIGHLY ANTICIPATED INSTRUMENTAL RELEASE THAT MICHAEL HAS DESCRIBED AS "A SOUNDTRACK FOR THE MOVIES IN MY MIND," IS AVAILABLE FROM REUNION RECORDS. RECORDED PARTIALLY IN DUBLIN WITH THE FAMED IRISH FILM ORCHESTRA, FREEDOM FEATURES LUSH STRINGS BEHIND MICHAEL'S MOVING PIANO PLAYING THAT BRINGS TO LIFE THE ALBUM'S SWEEPING BALLADS. ON THE CD IN THIS BOOK, YOU CAN ENJOY THE SINGLE FREEDOM TWO WAYS——THE ORIGINAL INSTRUMENTAL AND THE EXCLUSIVE RECORDING WITH PATRIOTIC QUOTATIONS.

ALSO FROM MICHAEL W. SMITH, THE BOOK WORSHIP, IN WHICH MICHAEL REFLECTS ON THIS VITAL PART OF THE CHRISTIAN FAITH. THE BOOK INCLUDES AN ENHANCED CD WITH THE SINGLE BREATHE FROM MICHAEL'S HIT LIVE ALBUM WORSHIP ALSO FROM REUNION RECORDS.